D1266142

Barry Bonds

By Jeff Savage

AMAZING ATHLETES

LERNER**SPORTS** / **Minneapolis**

For Joshua Edwards, who may break Barry's records someday.

This book is available in two editions:
Library binding by LernerSports
Soft cover by First Avenue Editions
Imprints of Lerner Publishing Group
241 First Avenue North
Minneapolis, MN 55401 U.S.A.

Website address: www.lernerbooks.com

Library of Congress Cataloging-in-Publication Data

Savage, Jeff.
     Barry Bonds / by Jeff Savage.
        p.   cm. — (Amazing athletes)
     Includes index.
     Summary: Examines the personal life and career of the San Francisco Giants baseball player who holds the record for most home runs in a season and is the first baseball player to win five MVP awards.
     ISBN: 0–8225–3688–9 (lib. bdg. : alk. paper)
     ISBN: 0–8225–2037–0 (pbk. : alk. paper)
     1. Bonds, Barry, 1964—Juvenile literature. 2. Baseball players—United States—Biography—Juvenile literature. [1. Bonds, Barry, 1964– 2. Baseball players. 3. African Americans—Biography.] I. Title. II. Series.
GV865.B63S37 2004
796.357'092—dc22
                                                                    2003016548

Manufactured in the United States of America
1 2 3 4 5 6 – DP – 09 08 07 06 05 04

TABLE OF CONTENTS

Barry stands for the National Anthem at the 2002 World Series.

WORLD SERIES STAR

Barry Bonds stepped into the **batter's box.**
Hundreds of camera bulbs flashed around the
stadium. The fans at Edison Field in Anaheim,
California, knew the importance of the
moment. The San Francisco Giants were

facing the Anaheim Angels in Game One of the 2002 **World Series.** Barry had set many hitting records, including the most **home runs** in a season. Some people were calling Barry the greatest player in baseball history. But in seventeen **major league** seasons, there was one thing Barry sorely missed. He had never played in the World Series. This was Barry's first World Series **at-bat.**

"A dream came true, finally," Barry said beforehand. "I finally made it to 'the Game.'"

Barry let the first two pitches from Jarrod Washburn go by for **balls.** Barry then swung and missed for a **strike.** On Washburn's next pitch, Barry crushed the baseball high and deep to right field. The Angels outfielders turned and watched the ball sail far over the fence for a home run.

Millions of television viewers saw Barry circle the bases and touch home plate. They saw him get high fives from his teammates in the dugout. Fans had seen this scene many times before but never in such an important game. Barry's home run in the second inning

Barry smashes a homer during the 2002 World Series against the Anaheim Angels.

Crossing home plate after a home run, Barry gives his usual sign of thanks. Barry homered in each of the first three series games.

gave the Giants a 1–0 lead, and they went on to win this first game of the series 4–3. Barry said he cared more about his team than himself.

"I worry about winning," he said. "I don't care about the homer. Right now, I just want to win a World Series."

Barry played outfield for the Junipero Serra High School Padres.

BOBBY'S BOY

Barry Lamar Bonds was born July 24, 1964. Like many boys growing up, Barry dreamed of being a professional athlete someday. Unlike most boys, however, Barry knew all along what sport he would play—baseball. And Barry had the team figured out too—the San Francisco Giants. Barry had good reasons for his choices. His father, Bobby Bonds, was a baseball player for the Giants. The family lived in San Carlos, California, just south of San Francisco.

Bobby Bonds was an outfielder for the San Francisco Giants from 1968 to 1974.

When Barry was four years old, his mother, Pat, would drive him and his younger brother, Ricky, to Candlestick Park, the Giants' park. Barry and Ricky would play in the clubhouse while the Giants and their opponents were competing on the field. Barry would go from locker to locker, taking sticks of gum. He would stuff them into his mouth until he was chewing on a giant wad, just like the pros.

When Barry turned five, he got to wear a little Giants uniform and play on the field with his glove. During batting practice, he stood between his dad, who was in right field, and the center fielder, Willie Mays, to help **shag flies.**

Mays is one of the greatest players of all time and is also Barry's godfather. Bobby Bonds was a great player too. He combined power and speed to hit 30 or more home runs and **steal** 30 or more bases in the same season five times— more than anyone else ever.

Willie Mays, the Say Hey Kid, was a Giants superstar. He was inducted into the Baseball Hall of Fame in 1979.

Barry did not always fit in with his teammates.

As Barry grew older, he found it wasn't easy to be the son of a great player. At Serra High School, Barry played outfield. His teammates teased him by calling him "Bobby." Barry didn't let the teasing stop him from performing. He batted .467 and led Serra High to three straight championships.

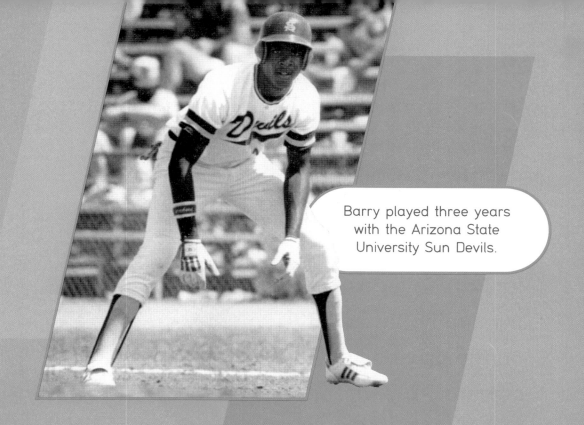

Barry played three years with the Arizona State University Sun Devils.

ON TO THE BIG LEAGUES

Barry had always planned to go to college. When he was a senior in high school, the Giants selected him in the second round of the 1982 **draft.** The team offered him $75,000 to sign a **contract** to play for its **minor league** team.

But Barry knew the importance of going to college, so he turned down the Giants' offer. He attended Arizona State University and played for the school team, the Sun Devils.

Living in the Arizona desert was different for Barry. He missed California and his family. But he felt comfortable on the playing field. In his sophomore year, the Sun Devils reached the College World Series. Barry tied a college record by getting seven straight hits in the series.

Barry fires back a fielded ball during a Sun Devils game.

Barry began piling up home runs with the Pittsburgh Pirates.

As a junior, he clubbed 23 home runs. After that, Barry decided he was ready for pro baseball. He declared himself eligible for the 1985 major league draft.

Barry was the sixth player picked in the draft. He was chosen by the Pittsburgh Pirates. Before Barry could play for the big-league club in Pittsburgh, Pennsylvania, he had to prove himself in the minor leagues.

Barry played outfield with the minor league team in Prince William, Virginia. He batted .299 with 13 home runs and 15 stolen bases. He joined the Pirates midway through the following season. In Barry's first game, he hit a **double** against the Los Angeles Dodgers.

Five days later, against the Atlanta Braves, he slugged his first home run. Barry kept right on hitting. He finished the season leading all rookies with 16 homers, 48 **runs batted in** (RBIs), and 36 stolen bases.

In February 1988, Barry married a young Swedish woman named Sun, short for Susann.

Barry's second season was even better. He clubbed 25 home runs, scored 99 runs, and stole 32 bases. People were starting to believe Barry would be as good as his father.

After seven years with the Pirates, though, everyone realized that Barry was even better. In his final seasons in Pittsburgh, Barry was named the most valuable player (MVP) in the National League twice, in 1990 and 1992. He led Pittsburgh to the **playoffs** in 1990, 1991, and 1992. But each time, the Pirates fell just short of reaching the World Series.

Barry's slugging led the Pirates to the playoffs three years in a row.

When Barry joined the Giants, he took number 25, the number Bobby *(center)* wore with the team. Willie Mays *(left)* joined them for the 1993 signing ceremony.

A GIANT STAR

In 1993, Barry became a **free agent.** He could join any team that wanted him. The San Francisco Giants offered Barry a contract. Barry immediately signed it. The contract was for six years and $44 million. *Forty-four million dollars.*

Barry could hardly believe it. It was the richest contract in all of sports. Before long, however, the Giants were saying that they got a bargain.

Barry did not like playing at Candlestick Park. A cold wind howled past him in left field. Even routine fly balls were difficult to catch. But Barry stayed focused.

Candlestick Park was notorious for its cold winds.

The Bonds family poses for a fan. Barry and his second wife, Liz, sit behind (left to right) Nikolai, Aisha, and Shikari.

He routinely won the Gold Glove Award, given each year to the best fielder at each position. Even better, in his first season with the Giants, he won the National League MVP award for the third time. But the Giants missed making the playoffs on the last day of the season.

Barry had ups and downs in his personal life too. He and his wife, Sun, decided to divorce in 1994. But they agreed to share the care of son Nikolai and daughter Shikari. He would later marry Liz Watson, with whom he has a daughter named Aisha.

In 1998, Barry won his eighth Gold Glove Award as a National League outfielder.

Pitchers sometimes throw four balls on purpose to send power hitters to first base, rather than risk letting them get a hit. In 1999, Barry was given his 293rd walk on purpose, matching Hank Aaron for the most in Major League history.

Over the next three years, Barry smacked 37, 33, and 42 home runs. He had become the most feared hitter in baseball. The trouble was, the Giants kept missing the playoffs. That changed in 1997. Barry led the Giants to their first playoff appearance in eight years. But Barry's team fell short of the World Series—again. The Giants reached the playoffs again in 1999. Again they came up short. Would Barry ever play in a World Series?

Pacific Bell Park overlooks McCovey Cove, part of San Francisco Bay.

BREAKING RECORDS

In 2000, the Giants had a new home. They moved from Candlestick Park to brand-new Pacific Bell Park. The players were thrilled with their beautiful new stadium. Barry hit a career high 49 homers, many of them splashing into San Francisco Bay beyond the right-field fence.

Barry continued his power hitting into 2001. The record for the most home runs in one season had stood for three years. In 1998, Mark McGwire of the St. Louis Cardinals hit 70 home runs. That same year, Sammy Sosa of the Chicago Cubs hit 66. Their feats shattered Roger Maris's record of 61 home runs.

But in 2001, Barry Bonds topped them both. He smashed a record 73 home runs!

Barry and godfather Willie Mays showed their emotions in a postgame ceremony marking Barry's 71st home run.

As Barry waits in the outfield for a play, a sign heralds his landmark home run. Barry hit his 500th homer on April 17, 2001.

Barry was chosen as the National League's 2001 MVP. It was his fourth MVP award, more than any other player in history. Barry called his record-breaking year "meaningful." But what he really wanted was to play in a World Series. In 2002, Barry finally got his wish. The Giants defeated the Braves and the St. Louis Cardinals in the playoffs to reach the World Series.

The Giants and Anaheim Angels battled to win the World Series. The team that won four games first would be champion. The Giants won the first game, the Angels won the next two, and the Giants won the next two. The Giants needed to win one more game.

On August 23, 2002, Barry hit his 600th home run. In joining the exclusive 600 club, Barry took his place next to Willie Mays *(left)* and Hank Aaron *(center)*.

In Game Six in Anaheim, the Giants took a 5–0 lead into the seventh inning. Barry had helped with a home run, his fourth of the series. Amazingly, though, the Angels rallied with three runs in the seventh inning and three in the eighth to win the game, 6–5. The Giants lost the deciding seventh game as well.

A Giants fan pins on a carnation in memory of Bobby Bonds. Bobby died in August 2003 after a battle with cancer.

It was a devastating way to end a special season. But Barry was the unanimous choice for the National League MVP.

In 2003, Barry overcame Bobby's death to lead the Giants to the playoffs again. This time they lost in the first round to the Florida Marlins. Along the way, Barry continued to bash home runs in pursuit of another great mark—Hank Aaron's record of 755 home runs. Will Aaron's record be broken? If anyone can do it, it's Barry Bonds.

In the 2003 postseason, Barry was named the National League MVP for the sixth time. He is the only player in major league history to receive the MVP award three years in a row and more than three times.

Selected Career Highlights

2003 Named the National League MVP for the sixth time
Played in his twelfth All-Star Game

2002 Named the National League MVP for the fifth time
Won the National League's batting title for the first time
Received his second National League Hank Aaron Award as best
  overall hitter in the league
Hit eight home runs during the playoffs and World Series, setting a
  single postseason record

2001 Named the National League MVP for a record fourth time
Broke baseball's all-time single-season home run record with 73
Received the National League Hank Aaron Award

2000 Won Major League Baseball's home run title

1996 Became the second player in history with 40 or more
  home runs and stolen bases in a single season

1993 Named the National League MVP for the
  third time
Won Major League Baseball's home run title
Led the National League in runs batted in

1992 Named the National League MVP for
  the second time

1990 Named the National League MVP
  for the first time
Played in his first All-Star Game

1989 Barry and his father Bobby
  broke the record for most
  career home runs by a
  father-son duo.

1986 Led National League rookies in
  home runs, runs batted in, and
  stolen bases

Glossary

at-bat: a batter's official turn at the plate during a game. If the batter walks, sacrifices, or is hit by a pitch, the turn is not counted as an at-bat.

balls: pitches that do not enter the strike zone and are not hit at by the batter

batter's box: a rectangular box drawn next to home plate. A batter must stand with both feet inside the box.

contract: an agreement that a player and team both sign. A contract states a player's salary and other details of the player's job with the team.

double: a play in which the batter hits the ball and safely reaches second base

draft: a yearly event in which all professional teams in a sport are given the chance to pick new players from a selected group. Most of the players in the group have played their sport in college.

free agent: a player whose contract with one team has ended, freeing him to join any team that offers to sign him

home runs: hits that allow batters to circle all the bases in one play to score a run

major league: a group of professional teams ranked highest in its sport

minor league: a league ranked below the major league, in which players improve their playing skills and prepare to move to the majors

playoffs: a series of games played after a regular season to determine which teams will play in a championship

runs batted in (RBIs): the number of runners able to score on a batter's hit, including the batter

shag flies: during batting practice, standing in the outfield to catch batted fly balls and throw them back to the pitcher

steal: when a runner on base advances to the next base without waiting for the batter to get a hit

strike: a pitch that enters the strike zone or is swung at but not hit fair by the batter

World Series: baseball's championship tournament. In Major League Baseball, the National and American Leagues hold playoffs at the end of the regular season. The winning teams from those playoffs meet in the World Series.

Further Reading & Websites

Dougherty, Terri. *Barry Bonds*. Edina, MN: Abdo & Daughters, 2002.

Miller, Raymond H. *Barry Bonds*. San Diego, CA: Kidhaven Press, 2002.

Muskrat, Carrie. *Barry Bonds*. Philadelphia, PA: Chelsea House, 1997.

Savage, Jeff. *Barry Bonds: Record Breaker*. Minneapolis, MN: LernerSports, 2002.

Thornley, Stew. *Super Sports Star Barry Bonds*. Berkeley Heights, NJ: Enslow Publishers, 2004.

Barry Bonds Central
<http://www.bondscentral.com>
This fan website features trivia, photos, videos, and other information about Barry Bonds.

Major League Baseball Website
<http://www.mlb.com>
This website developed by Major League Baseball provides fans with game action, biographies of players, and information about teams and baseball.

Sports Illustrated for Kids
<http:www.sikids.com>
The *Sports Illustrated for Kids* website covers all sports, including baseball.

Index

Photo Acknowledgments

Photographs are used with the permission of: © 2002 Rich Pilling/MLB Photos, p. 4; © 2002 Brad Mangin/MLB Photos, pp. 6, 7, 20; © Serra High School, pp. 8, 12; © Bettmann/CORBIS, pp. 10, 11; © Arizona State University, pp. 13, 14; © 1992 Chuck Solomon/MLB Photos, p. 15; © Getty Images, pp. 17, 23; © Mickey Pfleger/ENDZONE, p. 18; © National Baseball Hall of Fame, p. 19; © 1997 Don Smith/MLB Photos, p. 21; © Reuters NewMedia Inc./CORBIS, p. 24; © AFP/CORBIS, pp. 25, 26; © Susan Ragan/Reuters NewMedia Inc./Corbis, p. 27; 2002/MLB Photos, p. 29.

Cover: © AFP/Getty Images/Getty Images.